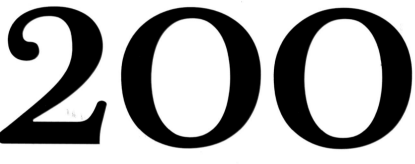

200

POTLUCK DISHES

MICHELLE KEOGH

SELLERS
PUBLISHING

A Quintet Book

Published by Sellers Publishing, Inc.
161 John Roberts Road, South Portland, Maine 04106
Visit our Web site: www.sellerspublishing.com
E-mail: rsp@rsvp.com

ISBN: 978-1-4162-4582-7
Library of Congress Control Number: 2016930065
QTT.RFSP

This book was conceived, designed and produced by
Quintet Publishing Limited
Ovest House
58 West Street
Brighton
BN1 2RA

Project Editor: Leah Feltham
Photographer: Tony Briscoe
Food Stylist: Julia Azzarello
Designer: Tania Gomes
Art Director: Michael Charles
Editorial Director: Emma Bastow
Publisher: Mark Searle

10 9 8 7 6 5 4 3 2 1

Printed in China by Toppan Leefung

CONTENTS

introduction

A potluck is a gathering of friends or family where each person contributes a dish to be shared. The name relates to an old practice of keeping a pot on the stove for all the leftover meats and vegetables to be thrown into. It was kept hot in case of unexpected guests, so that anyone who popped in could be offered some stew. Although this dish was always available, due to the random nature of the ingredients, what it tasted like depended on what was in the pot.

Potluck parties are easy to plan. Pick a time and place and instruct everyone to bring a dish — what you end up with is potluck! It makes for an interesting meal as you don't know what will be on offer, and a stress-free gathering as the cooking is shared equally among the guests. People can choose what to bring based on their own skills, food availability, and tastes, or the host can guide the event a little by instructing guests on the type of dish to bring, to make sure there is an even spread available. The host could even choose to guide the event with a theme; for example, a cultural style, such as Mexican or Italian; or a cooking style, such as barbecue; or even an ingredient or an era in time.

In this book you will find everything you need for your next potluck, whether you are attending as a guest, or hosting the whole event. From dips and appetizers, mains and salads, all the way through to sides and desserts, you are sure to find the perfect dish for your next gathering.

planning a potluck

Along with an invitation, whether formal or informal, it is often advisable to provide some guidelines for guests on what to bring along; this will help to avoid multiple people bringing the same dish, or an entire course being overlooked. This can be as general as instructing guests to bring a certain course — some guests could bring appetizers, others could bring mains, and so on — or as specific as listing the dishes. There are even lists online that you can use for guests to tell everyone else what they're bringing.

When hosting a potluck, try to have a variety of serving utensils and dishes on hand when guests arrive — serving utensils in particular can be easily overlooked. Generally, the host provides cutlery, plates, napkins, cups, and glasses. Whether these are disposable or not often depends on the size of the gathering. For a very large gathering, using the host's own items can be impractical, both in terms of having enough to go around and washing the dishes afterwards. Asking a guest or two to bring some of these items instead of food can be helpful.

Another thing to keep in mind, whether hosting or attending a potluck, is who's providing the drinks? The host should advise guests what they are planning to provide, and could ask them to bring other drinks based around this. For larger gatherings, where a little planning is involved, you can ask some guests to bring drinks instead of food, and ask others to increase the serving sizes of their food dishes. If alcohol is to be served, the host may choose to provide the basics of beer and wine and ask guests to bring other drinks if they would like to.

As potlucks tend to be informal gatherings, it's a good idea to have an open seating plan to encourage guests to mingle. Generally, food is set up as a buffet on a separate table without seating so guests can see everything that's on offer and choose what they would like to try, serving themselves. Placing the food tables in a low traffic area should help to prevent overcrowding, and placing plates at one end of the table and cutlery and napkins at the other can help channel guests into a line, as they will start at the plate end and work their way down the table to the other end. Placing the cutlery at the other end of the table ensures guests don't have to juggle them while they are trying to fill their plate. Having a designated table or area for drinks separate from the food area will also help to prevent overcrowding. All food may be put out together, or it may be put out as courses; appetizers and dips immediately; salads, sides, and mains together, and desserts last. This works well if there are a lot of cold or frozen desserts, as they can be kept in the refrigerator or freezer until guests are ready. If you are placing all dishes out at the same time, keeping similar courses together will help guests to choose, and ensure no dishes are overlooked.

Make sure bakes, bars, and sheet cakes are pre-cut into portions to allow guests to easily serve themselves. Encourage guests to think about the presentation of their dish; if a garnish or finishing touch won't travel well, it can be brought separately and put it on the dish just before serving. Leafy salads are best when dressed just before serving, as they tend to wilt and go soggy if left too long. Sprinkles and grated chocolate, or whipped cream garnishes, are also best applied just before serving. The same can be said of some chopped herbs, such as basil and mint, which tend to bruise and darken if left too long after chopping.

Providing pens and small pieces of paper so guests can write down the name of their dish and place it with the dish on the serving table is a great way of letting everyone know what's on offer; this can also be useful if there are guests with special dietary requirements.

attending a potluck

If you've been invited to a potluck, try to get an idea of what the host would like you to bring. It doesn't have to be specific, but even a general idea will help to ensure you are not bringing the same as another guest. Try to avoid dishes

that are extremely overpowering or spicy, or that are filled with overly unusual ingredients; the idea is to try to serve a dish that most people will enjoy.

Try to provide everything that will be needed to finish and serve your dish. If it's served hot, bring a trivet or towels to sit the dish on. Think about what serving utensils to bring, what to serve it on, and any final touches or garnishes that will make it more appealing. There are plates for some dishes, such as cakes and appetizers, that serve the double purpose of transporting them well and presenting them attractively for serving. If you are bringing a salad in a plastic container, perhaps bring along a serving bowl to transfer it to before serving, and some salad servers. These small things, while not necessary, can make the food on offer look more attractive and appealing, and therefore, enjoyable.

how many dishes?

The dishes on offer should be spread evenly across the categories of dips and appetizers, salads, mains, sides, and desserts. In a potluck of ten people, two could bring a dish from one category, two could bring a dish from another, and so on. This way, you will end up with a good variety of food, and if someone can't make it, there should still be another

option. For this size gathering, if each dish serves six to eight people, there should be enough for everyone to have a full-size portion in each category, or a small portion of each dish, with plenty left for second helpings.

Allocating categories evenly between guests should also work well for larger gatherings, if everyone is bringing a dish. The portion sizes would be a lot smaller, but the variety would be far greater. If the guests attending are mostly couples and bringing a dish between them, then doubling or tripling recipe quantities is advisable. A good guide is to make enough of each dish to feed most, but not all, of the guests a small portion.

increasing recipe quantities

Most recipes can be scaled up to suit the size of the gathering. Generally, for larger dishes, simply doubling or tripling the recipe will work. It can be helpful to work out the ingredient amounts and write them down before you begin; if you are calculating in your head you may accidently revert back to the original amounts.

For cooked dishes, pan and pot sizes will need to be increased accordingly and cooking times may lengthen, as larger volumes of food will take longer to heat up, and therefore cook. The best way to deal with this is to follow the original cooking times, check the dish when it would normally be cooked, and if it's not done re-check the dish every five to ten minutes until it is. The usual methods of checking for doneness can be helpful here. Cakes should spring back when gently pressed with a finger, and a skewer inserted into the center should come out clean. Vegetables should be tender. Meats should be firm to touch — using a meat thermometer is a helpful way to check for doneness in large whole pieces of meat, whereas texture and tenderness are signs to look for in casseroles and stews. When doubling recipes for cakes and breads, it is usually best to make two regular ones, rather than one double-sized one. Recalculating pan sizes, cooking times, and temperatures can be a little tricky for these and may give inconsistent results.

food safety and transportation

A concern at any potluck is food safety, as food is often prepared and heated hours in advance of serving. The longer food is kept at dangerous temperatures (40–140°F/4–60°C), the greater the risk of harmful bacteria and microorganisms growing and causing a food-borne illness. Storing foods correctly until it's time to serve them will greatly reduce the risk of illness.

Once you have decided what to prepare, plan how it will be cooked, stored, and transported. Contact the host in advance if you will require refrigerator, freezer, stove, or oven space when you arrive. Refrigerated dishes need to be kept below 40°F (4°C), so keep them in the refrigerator until it's time to move them. Use ice or icepacks in insulated coolers to keep them cold while in transit. When you arrive at your destination, store them in the refrigerator until it's time to serve.

Frozen dishes can be tricky to transport, especially in warmer weather. Preparing your frozen dish at least 48 hours in advance will ensure that it is frozen hard all the way through. If you can, freezing at 0°F (–18°C) will help the dish stay frozen longer. Transport frozen dishes in the same way as refrigerated, using plenty of ice or icepacks in an insulated cooler. Check whether there will be a freezer available for use at the potluck venue; if not, try adding extra insulation by wrapping blankets or towels around the cooler.

For hot dishes, the safest option is to prepare them to the point of cooking in advance, and then store them below 40°F (4°C) until it's time to cook just before serving. Another option is to completely cook the dish in advance, cool it quickly to below 40°F (4°C), and re-heat it to above 140°F (60°C) before serving. The partial cooking of food, particularly meat, poultry, fish, and eggs, is not recommended as the food spends far too long at dangerous temperatures.

If there are no facilities available at the destination, cook your dish as close as possible to traveling time. Try to use ceramic or cast-iron cookware, as they will retain far more heat than thinner materials. Once cooked, cover the dish and wrap it in aluminum foil and newspapers, blankets, or towels for insulation during the journey. As heat rises, it pays to add extra insulation to the top of the dish. It is also possible to buy insulated bags and heat packs for transporting hot food. Whatever you use, have it ready before the dish is finished cooking, this way the hot dish won't be sitting getting cold while you organize it. Once food has been served at the gathering, it should not be left out for longer than two hours. After this, foods that would normally be stored in the refrigerator should be discarded.

If you are hosting the potluck, try to find out in advance which guests will require refrigerator or freezer space on arrival, and which will require space in the oven or on the stove. Having the oven pre-heated for guests' arrival will ensure that food can be placed straight into it, lessening time delays. Try to ensure there's plenty of refrigerator and freezer space available. It's easier and safer to store drinks in insulated coolers or tubs of ice, so use these to keep drinks cool and reserve the refrigerator and freezer for food.

Keep in mind that some dishes just may not be practicable for some potlucks, particularly those that won't keep hot when there are no cooking facilities at the destination. Try to choose a dish that can be completely prepared in advance, is easy to transport, and doesn't require too much difficulty to serve.

meat temperatures

It is important to cook meat and poultry to high enough internal temperatures to kill any harmful bacteria inside. The color of the meat is not always the best indicator of it being cooked. The failsafe way of checking for doneness is by using a food thermometer. Food thermometers for this purpose consist of a metal probe with a temperature gauge at one end. Inserting the metal probe into the middle of the thickest part of the dish will give you a reliable indicator of whether the meat is safely cooked. It's always best to check the temperature of a few different areas in the dish, as foods can cook unevenly, due to thickness, density, and uneven cooking temperatures.

The following is a guide to safe internal temperatures for different types of meat.

SAFE INTERNAL TEMPERATURES FOR MEAT	
Ground beef, pork, veal, and lamb	160°F (71°C)
Ground chicken and turkey	165°F (74°C)
Fresh beef, pork, veal, lamb, and ham	145°F (63°C)
Fresh chicken and turkey	165°F (74°C)
Fish	145°F (63°C)

dips & appetizers

These flavor-loaded dips and appetizers are bound to be popular. You'll find a variety of dishes here that will whet the appetite.

guacamole

A potluck classic, guacamole is sure to be a favorite at any party. Serve with corn chips or fresh tortillas for dipping.

3 large, ripe avocados
juice of 1 lime
1/2 small red onion, finely chopped
1 medium tomato, finely chopped
1 small chile, finely chopped
2 tbsp. finely chopped fresh cilantro
salt and freshly ground black pepper

Serves 6–8

Cut the avocados in half, running the knife lengthwise around the pit. Twist the two halves away from each other and use a teaspoon to remove the pit. Use a spoon to scoop the avocado flesh into a mixing bowl.

Add the lime juice to the avocado and mash them together with a fork until the avocado is fairly smooth, but some texture remains.

Add the red onion, tomato, chile, and cilantro. Stir to combine and season to taste with salt and pepper. Spoon the guacamole into a serving dish, cover with plastic wrap, and refrigerate until ready to serve.

NOW TRY THIS

guacamole with lemon & parsley
Prepare the basic recipe, replacing the lime juice with the juice of half a lemon, and the cilantro with 2 tablespoons chopped fresh parsley.

guacamole with goat cheese
Prepare the basic recipe, stirring in 2 ounces crumbled goat cheese with the tomato, onion, chile, and cilantro.

layered mexican dip
Prepare the guacamole as directed. In a 7-inch (18-cm) glass serving bowl, layer one 15-ounce can of rinsed and drained black beans, 1 cup thawed frozen corn kernels, 2 chopped tomatoes, the guacamole, and 4 ounces grated cheddar or Monterey Jack cheese. Chill until ready to serve.

minty cucumber & yogurt dip

This refreshing dip, based on the classic Greek tzatziki, makes a perfect light, informal appetizer. Serve it with pita bread or chips for scooping.

1 large cucumber
2 cups Greek yogurt
2 garlic cloves, crushed
1/4 cup chopped fresh mint
salt
Serves 8

Peel the cucumber, cut it in half lengthwise, and scrape out the seeds. Grate it and place it in a sieve. Press out as much liquid as possible.

Place the cucumber in a bowl and mix in the yogurt, garlic, and mint. Season to taste with salt. Transfer to a serving bowl and chill until ready to serve.

NOW TRY THIS

garlicky cucumber & yogurt dip
Prepare the basic recipe, adding an extra 2 cloves of crushed garlic.

spicy cucumber & yogurt dip
Prepare the basic recipe, adding 2 seeded and finely chopped green chiles.

mixed herb & cucumber dip
Prepare the basic recipe, adding 2 tablespoons snipped fresh chives and 2 tablespoons chopped fresh cilantro with the mint.

beet crisps

Colorful crisps made from wafer-thin slices of beet are easy to make and are great with drinks. Serve them on their own or with a little bowl of creamy dip.

2–4 fresh beets
sunflower oil, for deep-frying
Course sea salt, for sprinkling

Serves 8

Trim and peel the beets, then use a mandolin or vegetable peeler to slice them into thin shavings. Rinse well, then pat dry with paper towels.

Pour enough sunflower oil into a pan to fill it about one-third full and heat to 375°F (190°C), or until a cube of bread added to the pan turns golden in about 1 minute.

Working in batches, deep-fry the beet slices for about 1 minute, until crisp. Lift the beets out of the oil using a slotted spoon and drain them on a wire rack covered with several layers of paper towels. Sprinkle with salt and serve.

NOW TRY THIS

parsnip crisps
Use 2 to 4 parsnips in place of the beets to make sweet, golden crisps.

pumpkin crisps
To make rich, orange crisps, use a large wedge of pumpkin in place of the beets.

mixed vegetable crisps
Make multicolored crisps by using a mixture of root vegetables, such as beets, sweet potato, and potato.

deviled eggs

This retro classic is a fun way to spice up any gathering. It's also simple to prepare and easy to serve. The eggs can be boiled a day in advance, refrigerated, and then filled on the day of the party.

6 large eggs
2 tbsp. mayonnaise
1 tsp. yellow mustard
salt and freshly ground black pepper
paprika, to serve

Makes 12

Put the eggs in a medium saucepan and fill with cold water to cover the eggs by 1 inch (2.5 cm). Bring the water to a rolling boil and cook for 1 minute. Remove the pan from the heat, cover, and let sit for 10 minutes. Drain the eggs and leave them under cold running water until cool.

Peel the eggs and halve them lengthwise. Carefully remove the yolks, leaving the whites intact. Put the yolks in a small mixing bowl and mash them with a fork until smooth.

Add the mayonnaise and yellow mustard to the yolks and mix well. Season the mixture with salt and pepper, to taste.

Using a teaspoon, carefully fill the egg whites with the egg-yolk mixture. Alternatively, pipe the filling into the eggs. Cover with plastic wrap and store in the refrigerator for up to a day before using. Sprinkle the eggs lightly with paprika just before serving.

NOW TRY THIS

deviled eggs with ham
Add 1 ounce finely chopped ham to the mashed egg yolks, along with the mayonnaise and mustard.

deviled eggs with caviar
Top each deviled egg with 1/4 teaspoon caviar just before serving.

spiced deviled eggs
Add 1/4 to 1/2 teaspoon cayenne pepper to the yolk mixture, depending on how hot you like it.

herbed deviled eggs
Add 2 tablespoons of fresh herbs, such as parsley and chives, to the yolk mixture.

ham & cheese tortilla pinwheels

These delicious appetizers are always popular, and the filling can be varied easily with whatever you have on hand. Chilling the rolled tortillas overnight before slicing allows the filling to set and the flavors to develop.

4 oz. cream cheese, softened
1/4 cup sour cream
1/2 tsp. garlic powder
salt, to taste
1/2 tsp. freshly ground black pepper
2 tbsp. chopped fresh parsley
4 oz. sharp cheddar cheese, grated
4 (10-in./25-cm.) flour tortillas
8 thin slices deli ham

Serves 6–8

Combine the softened cream cheese, sour cream, garlic powder, salt and pepper in a mixing bowl and beat well with a fork to combine. Stir in the chopped parsley and cheese.

Lay the tortillas flat and spread them with the cream cheese mixture so each one is covered with an even layer. Arrange two slices of ham on each tortilla, and then roll each one up tightly. Wrap each tortilla tightly in plastic wrap, twisting the ends to secure them, and chill for at least 4 hours, or overnight.

Just before serving, remove the rolled tortillas from the plastic wrap and slice them into 1-inch- (2.5-cm-) thick rounds. Arrange the pinwheels on a serving platter, securing them with a toothpick, if needed.

NOW TRY THIS

pesto & feta tortilla pinwheels
Replace the cream cheese filling with 1/2 cup softened cream cheese mixed with 2 tablespoons sour cream and 3 tablespoons basil pesto, 1/2 cup grated sharp cheese and 1/4 cup crumbled feta cheese. Complete as before.

chile & olive tortilla pinwheels
Prepare the basic recipe, adding 1 large, hot red chile, finely chopped. Omit the ham and replace it with 1 cup chopped black olives.

confetti tortilla pinwheels
Omit the ham. Stir 1/2 cup thawed frozen corn kernels, 1 seeded and chopped tomato, 12 chopped black olives, and 1 finely sliced scallion into the cream cheese mixture.

baked spinach & artichoke dip

This delicious, hot dip is perfect served with fresh, crusty bread or tortilla chips. It can be prepared ahead and chilled until you are ready to bake.

1 cup frozen spinach, thawed

1 (14-oz.) can artichoke hearts, drained and coarsely chopped

4 oz. cream cheese, softened

1 cup mayonnaise

2 oz. Parmesan, grated

salt and freshly ground black pepper

2 oz. sharp cheddar cheese, grated

Serves 6–8

Preheat the oven to 375°F (190°C) and lightly grease a 9-inch- (23-cm-) square baking dish.

Use your hands to squeeze some of the excess moisture from the thawed spinach. Put the spinach in a mixing bowl with the artichoke hearts.

Put the softened cream cheese in a mixing bowl, add the mayonnaise and beat gently to combine.

Add the cream cheese mixture to the spinach and artichokes, along with the grated Parmesan, and stir until combined. Season the mixture with salt and pepper and pour it into the baking dish.

Sprinkle the sharp cheese over the dip and bake for 15 to 20 minutes, until the cheese is golden and the dip is just bubbling. Serve immediately.

NOW TRY THIS

baked spinach & sun-dried tomato dip
Prepare the basic recipe, replacing the artichokes with 2 cups sun-dried tomatoes, drained and roughly chopped.

baked arugula & artichoke dip
Prepare the basic recipe, replacing the spinach with 1 cup chopped arugula.

baked spinach & artichoke dip with bacon
Finely chop 4 strips of bacon and fry until crispy. Drain the bacon on paper towels before adding it to the spinach and artichokes with the cream cheese and mayonnaise.

fiery pumpkin dip

This glorious orange dip offers a rich combination of sweet, spicy, fiery, and sour flavors. Be warned, once you start dipping, it's hard to stop.

2 lb. 6 oz. pumpkin or butternut squash, seeded, peeled, and cut into chunks

1/4 cup olive oil, divided

salt and freshly ground black pepper

2 garlic cloves

2 tsp. grated ginger

2 red chiles, seeded and finely chopped

juice of 1 lime

Serves 8

Preheat the oven to 400°F (200°C). Put the pumpkin or squash in a baking dish, drizzle with 2 tablespoons of the oil, and season with salt and pepper. Roast for about 20 minutes, until tender, tossing once or twice during cooking.

Transfer the pumpkin or squash into a food processor and add the garlic, ginger, chile, and remaining oil. Process until smooth, then briefly pulse in the lime juice and check the seasoning.

Transfer the dip into a serving bowl and serve hot, warm, or cold. It will thicken on cooling, so give it a good stir before serving. Serve with pita bread, tortilla chips, or beet crisps (see page 13).

NOW TRY THIS

chunky pumpkin dip
Instead of using a food processor, coarsely mash the squash or pumpkin by hand and stir in the other ingredients to produce a chunkier dip.

curried pumpkin dip
Prepare the basic recipe, adding 2 teaspoons medium curry paste to the cooked pumpkin and the juice of 1 to 2 lemons instead of the lime juice.cheddar

spicy pumpkin dip with harissa
Prepare the basic recipe, omitting the chile and adding 2 teaspoons harissa (hot chile paste) and 2 teaspoons ground cumin instead.

deep-fried risotto balls

These rich, creamy risotto balls filled with basil and melting mozzarella are an indulgent feast of an appetizer. Serve them with fresh, tangy tomato or fruit salsa.

1/4 cup olive oil

2 small onions, finely chopped

2 garlic cloves, crushed

1 1/3 cups risotto rice

2/3 cups white wine

3 1/3 cups boiling vegetable or chicken stock

2 1/2 oz. grated Parmesan cheese

1/4 cup chopped fresh flat-leaf parsley

salt and freshly ground black pepper

6 oz. mozzarella, cut into 24 small cubes

24 large basil leaves

sunflower oil, for deep-frying

Serves 8

Heat the olive oil in a large pan, then gently fry the onion and garlic for about 4 minutes, until soft but not brown. Add the rice, stir for 2 minutes, pour in the wine and simmer, stirring until the wine is absorbed. Add the stock and stir frequently for about 20 minutes, until the stock is absorbed and the risotto is creamy. Stir in the Parmesan, parsley and seasoning. Let cool.

Divide the cooled rice into 24 portions. Wrap each cube of mozzarella in a basil leaf. Press a portion of rice around each cube. Place on a board and let stand for at least 30 minutes. Pour sunflower oil into a deep pan until it is two-thirds full. Heat the oil to 375°F (190°C), or until a cube of bread added to the pan turns brown in about 1 minute. Deep-fry the risotto balls in batches for about 3 minutes, until crisp and golden. Drain on paper towels and serve hot.

NOW TRY THIS

deep-fried risotto balls with chives
Prepare the basic recipe, adding 1/4 cup snipped fresh chives in place of the parsley. Omit the basil leaves from the filling.

deep-fried herbed risotto balls
Prepare the basic recipe, stirring 1/4 cup snipped fresh chives and 1/4 cup chopped fresh mint into the risotto with the parsley.

deep-fried risotto balls with melting blue cheese
Prepare the basic recipe, using cubes of blue cheese in place of the mozzarella. Omit the basil leaves from the filling.

mozzarella & basil quesadilla wedges

Serve these warm wedges of melted cheese on their own or pair them with a tangy, zingy salsa for dipping.

olive oil, for brushing

4 large soft flour tortillas

10 oz. mozzarella cheese, thinly sliced

dried chili flakes, for sprinkling

2 handfuls of fresh basil leaves

Makes 24 small pieces

Brush or coat a large, non-stick skillet with olive oil and place over a medium heat. Lay 1 tortilla in the pan and arrange half the cheese on top. Sprinkle with a good pinch or two of chili flakes and half the basil leaves. Lay a second tortilla on top.

Cook for 1 to 2 minutes, until the tortilla is crisp and golden underneath. Then carefully flip it over and cook for a further 1 to 2 minutes, until crisp and golden on the second side.

Keep the quesadilla warm while you repeat the steps above with the remaining ingredients to make a second quesadilla. Slide both onto a board, and cut each into 12 wedges.

NOW TRY THIS

hot jalapeño quesadilla wedges
Prepare the basic quesadilla recipe, using 1/4 cup sliced jalapeños from a jar in place of the dried chili and basil leaves.

mozzarella quesadilla wedges with roasted bell pepper, basil & chili
Prepare the basic quesadilla recipe, adding 4 sliced roasted bell peppers with the basil and chili.

mozzarella & sun-dried tomato quesadilla wedges
Slice 8 drained sun-dried tomatoes. Prepare the basic quesadilla recipe, sprinkling on sun-dried tomatoes in place of the basil leaves.

salads

The perfect way to showcase fresh produce, salads can be as light and simple as a few ingredients, or hearty enough to make a meal. They're a great way to bring some variety to a potluck.

summery corn salad

This delicious salad is a rainbow of colors and is sure to stand out from the crowd at your next get-together. The abundance of fresh ingredients means it will taste as good as it looks.

5 ears of corn

2 large tomatoes, chopped

1 large green bell pepper, seeded and chopped

1 large red onion, chopped

1 large cucumber, chopped

2 tbsp. chopped fresh basil

for the dressing

1/4 cup olive oil

1/4 cup balsamic vinegar

1 tbsp. whole-grain mustard

1/2 tsp. salt

1/2 tsp. freshly ground black pepper

Serves 6–8

Boil the corn in lightly salted water for 5 minutes, or until tender. Drain the corn and put it under running water to cool. Once cooled, stand the corn upright on a chopping board, and holding it at the top with one hand, use a sharp knife to cut downward where the corn joins the cob to remove the kernels. Put the kernels in a large salad bowl.

Add the tomatoes, green pepper, red onion, cucumber, and basil to the corn.

Put the dressing ingredients in a small, airtight container and shake well to combine. Just before serving, pour the dressing over the salad and toss it gently to coat.

NOW TRY THIS

charred corn salad
Rather than boiling, lightly oil and broil each ear of corn until it is charred and cooked. Let cool before completing the recipe.

corn & avocado salad
Prepare the basic recipe, adding the chopped flesh of two ripe avocados to the tomatoes, pepper, onion, and cucumber.

mexican corn salad
Omit the basil and replace it with 2 tablespoons freshly chopped cilantro. Replace the dressing with one made from 3 tablespoons lime juice, 1/4 cup olive oil, 1 teaspoon ground cumin, 1 finely chopped chile, 1/2 teaspoon salt, and 1/2 teaspoon freshly ground black pepper.

southwestern pasta salad

Southwestern pasta salad is a potluck classic, and a must at any bring-a-plate gathering. Add the dressing just before serving.

4 1/2 cups short pasta, such as penne
1 tbsp. olive oil
1 large red bell pepper, seeded and chopped
1 large green bell pepper, seeded and chopped
4 scallions, finely sliced
1 (15 oz.) can of black beans, drained and rinsed
2 cups frozen corn kernels, thawed
1/2 cup coarsely chopped fresh cilantro

for the dressing
1/4 cup olive oil
juice of 1 lemon
1 red chile, finely chopped
1 clove garlic, crushed
2 tsp. ground cumin
1/2 tsp. salt
1/4 tsp. freshly ground black pepper

Serves 6–8

Cook the pasta as directed on the package, drain and leave it under cold, running water until it has cooled. Drain thoroughly and toss gently with the olive oil to prevent the pasta sticking together. Set aside.

Combine the pasta, red and green peppers, scallions, black beans, corn, and cilantro in a large serving bowl.

Place all the dressing ingredients in a small, airtight container and shake until well combined.

Pour the dressing over the salad and toss it gently until all the ingredients are combined and coated with dressing. Serve immediately.

NOW TRY THIS

southwestern pasta salad with tuna
Add 2 cups cooked, flaked tuna to the finished salad and toss it through very gently.

southwestern couscous salad
Prepare the basic recipe, replacing the pasta with 2 1/2 cups couscous, cooked according to the package directions and cooled.

southwestern pasta salad with chicken
Arrange the salad on a large serving platter. Broil 3–4 chicken breasts until tender and cooked through, slice them thinly and arrange them over the salad.

roasted pumpkin & quinoa salad

This is a delightfully rustic salad, suitable for any occasion and equally delicious served warm or cold. Quinoa is a small, edible seed that is often used in place of grains; cook it according to package directions.

1 lb. pumpkin, chopped into 1-in. (2.5-cm.) cubes

3 tbsp. olive oil

3 cups cooked quinoa

1 small red onion, finely chopped

2 medium tomatoes, chopped

2 cups chopped fresh arugula

1/2 cup sliced olives

2 oz. crumbled feta

for the dressing

1/2 cup basil pesto

2 tbsp. white wine vinegar

2 tbsp. olive oil

Serves 6–8

Preheat the oven to 375°F (190°C). Put the pumpkin in a medium baking pan and drizzle with the olive oil. Bake it for 15 to 20 minutes, or until tender and golden. Set aside to cool.

Combine the quinoa, red onion, tomatoes, arugula, olives, and feta in a large serving bowl.

Prepare the dressing by putting the pesto, vinegar, and olive oil in a small mixing bowl and stirring until well combined.

Add the dressing to the salad, along with the roasted pumpkin, and toss gently until the ingredients are well mixed and coated in dressing.

NOW TRY THIS

broiled asparagus & quinoa salad
Prepare the basic recipe, replacing the pumpkin with 20 stalks of asparagus, brushed with olive oil, broiled, and cut into pieces.

roasted pepper & rice salad
Replace the pumpkin with 3 large red bell peppers that have been brushed with olive oil and roasted in a 400°F (200°C) oven for 10 to 15 minutes. Discard the skin and seeds and cut the flesh into strips. Replace the quinoa with 3 cups cooked rice.

chicken & quinoa salad
Prepare the basic recipe, replacing the pumpkin with 3 to 4 chicken breasts, cut into thin strips, brushed with olive oil, and then broiled until cooked through.

black bean confetti salad

As the name suggests, this salad is a confetti of color and flavor. With its Mexican flavors, it goes well alongside grilled meat, tortillas, and sour cream, making it ideal for a potluck barbecue.

2 (15-oz.) cans black beans, rinsed and drained

2 cups. frozen corn kernels, thawed

1 large white onion, chopped

1 large red bell pepper, seeded and chopped

1 large green bell pepper, seeded and chopped

1/4 cup chopped fresh cilantro

for the dressing

juice of 1 lime

3 tbsp. olive oil

2 tsp. ground cumin

1/2 tsp. salt

1/4 tsp. freshly ground black pepper

Serves 6–8

Put the black beans and corn kernels into a large serving bowl.

Add the onion, red and green pepper, and cilantro to the bowl.

Place the dressing ingredients into a small, airtight container and shake well to combine. Just before serving, pour the dressing over the salad and toss it gently to coat.

NOW TRY THIS

brown rice confetti salad
Prepare the basic recipe, replacing the black beans with 3 cups cooked brown rice.

spiced confetti salad
Prepare the basic recipe, adding 2 finely chopped red chiles and 1/2 teaspoon cayenne pepper (or to taste) to the dressing.

confetti salad with tuna
Prepare the basic recipe, adding 15 ounces cooked, flaked tuna to the salad ingredients in the bowl.

strawberry & spinach salad

This unusual combination works wonderfully when paired with creamy goat cheese and raspberry vinegar. It's a refreshing and sophisticated summer treat, and the perfect bring-along dish when strawberries are in season.

10 oz. fresh baby spinach leaves, washed and dried

15 medium strawberries, hulled and sliced

7 oz. soft goat cheese

5 oz. roasted, chopped almonds

for the dressing

1/4 cup olive oil

3 tbsp. raspberry vinegar

salt and freshly ground black pepper, to taste

Serves 6–8

Put the spinach on a large serving platter or in a large bowl. Distribute the strawberries evenly over the top. Crumble the goat cheese into small pieces and dot them over the spinach and strawberries. Sprinkle the almonds over the salad.

Put the olive oil, raspberry vinegar, and salt and pepper into a small, airtight container and shake until well combined. Drizzle the dressing over the salad just before serving.

NOW TRY THIS

watermelon & feta salad
Replace the strawberries and goat cheese with 13 ounces watermelon, chopped into 1-inch (2.5-cm) pieces and 7 ounces crumbled feta.

strawberry, spinach & avocado salad
Prepare the basic recipe, adding 2 sliced avocados to the salad with the strawberries and goat cheese.

strawberry, spinach & prosciutto salad
Prepare the basic recipe, replacing the goat cheese with 6 slices of prosciutto, torn into bite-size pieces.

watercress & apple salad with endive & bacon

The combination of slightly bitter greens with salty bacon, sharp apple, and sweet maple dressing is absolutely perfect in this light salad.

12 oz. watercress

2 heads Belgian endive, leaves separated

8 thick-cut bacon slices (or 10 regular slices)

2 apples, cored and cut into wedges

for the dressing

2 tbsp. pure maple syrup

6 tbsp. balsamic vinegar

1/2 cup grapeseed oil (or canola oil)

salt and freshly ground pepper

Serves 8

Put a bed of watercress on each salad plate. Arrange the endive leaves attractively on the watercress.

Cut each slice of bacon into thirds, then fry in a dry, non-stick skillet until crisp and brown. Remove the bacon from the skillet and let it drain on paper towels. Fry the apple wedges in the bacon grease on both sides until golden brown. Remove and drain on paper towels.

Mix the maple syrup with the balsamic vinegar and oil, then season to taste with salt and pepper. Sprinkle the dressing over the salad. Scatter the fried bacon and apple wedges on top and serve.

NOW TRY THIS

watercress & pear salad with endive & bacon
Prepare the basic recipe, using 2 pears in place of the apples. Peel and core the pears before slicing.

watercress, apple & celery salad
Prepare the basic recipe, replacing the endive with 8 sliced celery stalks.

watercress & apple salad with endive & walnuts
Prepare the basic recipe, omitting the bacon slices and leaving the apple wedges raw. Scatter 1/2 cup walnut pieces over the salad before serving.

country slaw

This crunchy and colorful slaw made with crisp raw vegetables has a simple, rustic feel. Make it in late summer when sweet peppers and tender zucchini are at their best.

4 stalks celery, thinly sliced
8 carrots, peeled and cut into matchsticks
4 zucchini, cut into matchsticks
4 red bell peppers, cut into thin strips
very large bunch fresh basil, chopped

for the dressing
1/4 cup white balsamic vinegar
1/4 cup lemon juice
2 tsp. honey
6 tbsp. grapeseed oil or canola oil
salt and freshly ground pepper
fresh basil leaves, to garnish

Serves 8

Put the celery, carrots, zucchini, bell peppers, and chopped basil into a large bowl.

In a small bowl, mix the balsamic vinegar with the lemon juice, honey, and oil. Pour the dressing over the vegetables, and toss to combine. Season to taste with salt and pepper. Serve in individual bowls, garnished with basil.

NOW TRY THIS

country slaw with honey-mustard dressing
Prepare the basic recipe, whisking 2 teaspoons Dijon mustard into the dressing.

country slaw with fresh oranges
Prepare the basic recipe. Cut away the peel from 4 oranges, then slice between the segments to release the flesh, and add to the salad.

country slaw with apple
Prepare the basic recipe, adding 2 cored, diced apples to the prepared vegetables.

tortellini salad

Tortellini salad is a hearty crowd-pleaser that can be made a day ahead of time and chilled. Store the dressing separately and dress the salad at the potluck before serving.

1 1/2 lb. spinach tortellini

1 tbsp. olive oil

2 large tomatoes, chopped

1 medium cucumber, chopped

1 medium red onion, finely chopped

1/2 cup sliced black olives

2 tbsp. chopped fresh parsley

for the dressing

1/2 cup mayonnaise

2 tbsp. white wine vinegar

Serves 6–8

Bring a large pan of lightly salted water to a rolling boil, add the tortellini and cook according to package directions. Once cooked, drain the tortellini and leave under cold, running water until it has cooled. Drain thoroughly and toss gently with the olive oil to prevent the pasta sticking together. Set aside.

Combine the tomatoes, cucumber, red onion, olives, and parsley in a large serving bowl.

Add the tortellini to the bowl and toss the salad gently until the ingredients are well combined. In a small bowl, mix together the mayonnaise and white wine vinegar. When you are ready to serve the salad, stir in the dressing until the ingredients are coated.

NOW TRY THIS

tortellini salad with crispy bacon
Finely chop 6 strips of bacon and fry until crisp. Let them cool on paper towels. Sprinkle the bacon pieces over the salad.

cheesy tortellini salad
Prepare the basic recipe, replacing the spinach tortellini with four-cheese tortellini and adding 4 ounces grated sharp cheese.

greek tortellini salad
Add 4 ounces crumbled feta to the salad with the other ingredients. Replace the dressing with one made from 1/4 cup olive oil, the juice of 1 lemon, 1/2 teaspoon crushed garlic, and 1 tablespoon fresh thyme leaves whisked together and seasoned with salt and ground black pepper.

broccoli salad

This salad can easily be prepared the day before you need it, and then chilled in an airtight container until required. Store the dressing separately and dress the salad just before serving.

8 strips of bacon, finely chopped

3 large heads broccoli, cut into bite-size pieces

4 scallions, finely sliced

3 oz. dark raisins

1/2 cup chopped fresh parsley

for the dressing

1/2 cup mayonnaise

1/4 cup balsamic vinegar

1 tsp. brown sugar

salt and freshly ground black pepper

Serves 6–8

Fry the bacon in a skillet over a medium-high heat until crisp and golden. Remove the bacon to some paper towels to drain.

Combine the broccoli, scallions, raisins, and parsley in a large serving bowl.

To make the dressing, put the mayonnaise, balsamic vinegar, and sugar into a bowl and beat until smooth.

Season the dressing with salt and pepper and pour it over the broccoli salad. Add the bacon pieces and toss gently until everything is well mixed and coated with dressing. Serve immediately.

NOW TRY THIS

cauliflower salad
Prepare the basic recipe, replacing the broccoli with one large head of cauliflower cut into small bite-size pieces.

creamy broccoli salad
Prepare the basic recipe, replacing the balsamic vinegar in the dressing recipe with 1/4 cup sour cream.

broccoli & cashew salad
Prepare the basic recipe, adding 1 cup roasted cashews to the salad with the bacon.

taco salad

This easy-to-serve salad combines all the flavors of traditional tacos.

2 tbsp. olive oil
1 lb. ground beef
1 tsp. chili powder
1/2 tsp. garlic powder
1/2 tsp. onion powder
1 tsp. paprika
1/2 tsp. cumin
1/2 tsp. dried oregano
1/3 cup water
salt and freshly ground black pepper
1 large iceberg lettuce, shredded
3 large tomatoes, cut into wedges
3 scallions, finely sliced
1/2 cup sliced black olives
1 cup grated, sharp Monterey Jack cheese
1 cup tomato salsa
1 (12 oz.) package corn chips

Serves 6–8

Place a large skillet over medium-high heat; add the olive oil and the ground beef. Cook the beef, stirring to break up lumps, until browned. Add the chili, garlic and onion powders, along with the paprika, cumin, and oregano, and toss the beef to coat it evenly. Add the water, reduce the heat to medium, and simmer until the moisture has been absorbed. Season with salt and freshly ground pepper, remove from the heat and let cool.

Layer the lettuce, tomatoes, and scallions on a large serving plate. Distribute the olives, cooled beef, and grated cheese over the top.

When you are ready to serve the salad, spoon the salsa over the beef and salad. Lightly crush a few corn chips and sprinkle over the top to garnish; put the rest in a serving bowl on the side. Serve immediately.

NOW TRY THIS

chicken taco salad
Replace the beef with 1 pound ground chicken, and continue as directed.

vegetarian taco salad
Replace the beef with two 15-ounce cans kidney beans, rinsed and drained. Fry gently for a few minutes with the olive oil, chili, garlic and onion powders, paprika, cumin, and oregano. Continue as directed. Ensure the cheese used is suitable for vegetarians.

taco salad with sour cream dressing
Replace the salsa with a dressing made by combining 1/2 cup sour cream with 1/2 cup mayonnaise, 1 ounce canned jalapeños, drained and chopped, and salt and freshly ground black pepper to taste.

mains

These crowd-pleasing main dishes are perfect for parties; easy to bring and serve, and totally delicious. Many can be prepared ahead to save you time later.

sticky bbq pork ribs

These sticky, tangy, melt-in-the-mouth ribs can be made ahead of time, up to the broiling stage, then broiled when you are ready to serve them.

4 lb. pork spare ribs

for the sauce

1 tbsp. olive oil

1 medium yellow onion, finely chopped

2 cloves garlic, finely chopped

1 cup ketchup

1/2 cup brown sugar

1/2 cup brown malt vinegar

1/2 cup maple syrup

1/2 cup dark soy sauce

salt and freshly ground black pepper

Serves 6–8

Preheat the oven to 350°F (175°C). Cut the racks of ribs into individual pieces and put them on a rack over a large baking pan lined with aluminum foil. Cover the ribs with aluminum foil and bake for 1 to 1 1/2 hours, until the meat is cooked and tender.

Put the olive oil in a medium saucepan over medium heat and sauté the onion and garlic for a few minutes, stirring occasionally, until they are translucent and beginning to color.

Add the remaining ingredients to the saucepan and bring to a boil. Reduce the heat and simmer the sauce for 5 minutes, until it has thickened slightly. Season with salt and pepper and remove from the heat.

Once the ribs are cooked, baste them liberally with the sauce and broil them on medium-high heat for another 15–20 minutes, turning and basting occasionally, until they are sticky, slightly charred and tender. Serve immediately with any remaining sauce on the side.

NOW TRY THIS

spiced bbq pork ribs
Prepare the basic recipe, adding 2 finely chopped hot red chiles with the onion and garlic. Add hot sauce to taste when seasoning with salt and pepper.

honey-mustard bbq pork ribs
Prepare the basic recipe, replacing the maple syrup with 1/2 cup honey. Reduce the malt vinegar to 1/4 cup and add 1/4 cup prepared yellow mustard to the sauce.

smoked bbq pork ribs
Prepare the basic recipe, adding 2 teaspoons liquid smoke to the sauce with the vinegar, maple syrup, and soy sauce.

sweet & spicy sticky chicken wings

The Chinese-inspired sauce for these chicken wings is made with hoisin sauce sweetened with brown sugar and spiced up with a little horseradish.

3 lbs. chicken wings

salt and freshly ground black pepper

canola oil, for deep-frying

for the sauce

1 cup hoisin sauce

1/2 cup cranberry juice

1/4 cup brown sugar

2 cloves garlic, finely chopped

1 tbsp. prepared horseradish

4 scallions, finely chopped

salt and freshly ground black pepper

Serves 6

Place the chicken wings on a baking sheet, and season both sides with salt and freshly ground black pepper. Set aside for 1 hour.

In a small pan, mix together all the sauce ingredients. Stirring continuously, bring to a boil. Reduce the heat to a simmer, and cook for about 20 minutes, until thickened, stirring frequently. Taste and adjust the seasoning.

In a large pan, over a medium-high heat, place enough canola oil to come half way up the sides, and using a thermometer, heat until it is 350°F (175°C). Deep-fry the wings in batches for about 6 minutes, or until golden brown and cooked through, turning them occasionally. Drain on paper towels. Put half the wings in a large bowl, add half of the sauce and toss together until well coated. Repeat with the rest of the wings and sauce. Refrigerate until required.

To reheat, spread the wings out on two large baking sheets and place on the grill for 10 minutes, until piping hot. Watch carefully to ensure they do not burn, turning them as necessary.

NOW TRY THIS

tamari & honey thighs
Slash 8 to 10 chicken thighs, and place them in a roasting pan. Mix 5 teaspoons vegetable oil, 1/4 cup tamari soy sauce, 6 tablespoons rice wine, 10 tablespoons chopped stem ginger in syrup, 6 crushed cloves garlic, and 3 to 4 chopped red chiles. Pour over the chicken and bake at 350°F (175°C) for 40 to 45 minutes. Drizzle with honey and broil for 3 minutes.

sweet & super spicy sticky chicken wings
Add 1 to 2 teaspoons crushed red chili flakes to the sauce. Alternatively, add a finely chopped red chile pepper if you like it really hot.

bacon & cheddar sliders

These baby hamburgers have that wonderful combination of bacon and cheddar cheese, and they are an ideal size to enjoy alongside other dishes.

12 oz. ground sirloin

3 shallots, finely chopped

1 tsp. Dijon mustard

salt and freshly ground black pepper

cooking spray

3 oz. grated cheddar cheese

8 whole-wheat slider buns

3 tbsp. mayonnaise

4 small dill pickles, cut lengthwise into 4 pieces

4 small lettuce leaves, each cut in half

1 ripe tomato, cut into 8 slices

3 slices bacon, cooked until crispy, and cut into 1-in. (2.5-cm.) pieces

Serves 8

Gently mix the sirloin with the shallots, Dijon mustard, salt and plenty of freshly ground black pepper. Divide into 8 portions and form into patties.

Spray the grill with cooking spray, and place the patties on the grill. Cook for 2 to 3 minutes on each side, topping each one with 1 tablespoon cheese during the last minute of cooking.

Spray the cut sides of the slider buns and grill until nicely toasted. Spread the bottom half of each bun with mayonnaise, add a patty, two slices of dill pickle, 1/2 lettuce leaf, 1 slice of tomato, and a pinch of bacon pieces. Season with freshly ground black pepper, and top with the other half of the slider buns. Serve immediately.

NOW TRY THIS

california sliders with guacamole
Omit the mayonnaise, dill pickles, lettuce, and bacon. Mash 2 avocados with the juice of 1/2 lime. Stir in 1 tablespoon freshly chopped cilantro, 1 minced clove garlic, 1/2 teaspoon salt, and 1/4 teaspoon cayenne pepper. Spread the slider buns with butter and grill as before. Assemble the sliders with the guacamole on top of the patties and cheese.

dixie burgers with chowchow dressing
Omit the dill pickles and bacon, and substitute chowchow dressing, made by mixing 1/2 cup chowchow (pickled relish) with 3 tablespoons mayonnaise.

cheesy broccoli rice

This is a super simple baked rice side that makes a versatile accompaniment to almost any savory dish. The rice can be prepared ahead of time up to the point the broth is added. Just add the broth and bake 40 minutes before you want to serve it.

3 tbsp. olive oil

1 medium yellow onion, finely chopped

1 clove garlic, finely chopped

2 cups long grain rice

2 small heads broccoli, cut into bite-size pieces

2 tbsp. chopped fresh oregano

5 cups hot vegetable broth

salt and freshly ground pepper

4 oz. grated sharp cheddar cheese

2 oz. grated Parmesan

Serves 6–8

Preheat the oven to 375°F (190°C). Set a large skillet over a medium-high heat, add the olive oil, onions, and garlic and sauté until translucent and beginning to color. Add the rice and toss it through the oil until it begins to look translucent.

Transfer the rice to a 7 x 10-inch (18 x 25-cm) baking dish and add the broccoli, oregano, and hot vegetable broth. Season with salt and pepper, cover the dish tightly with aluminum foil and bake for 30 to 35 minutes, or until all the moisture has been absorbed and the rice is tender.

Remove the foil and sprinkle the cheeses evenly over the top of the rice. Return the dish to the oven and bake until the cheese is melted and bubbling. Serve immediately.

NOW TRY THIS

cheesy bacon & cauliflower rice
Omit the broccoli from the basic recipe. Finely chop 4 strips of bacon and add them to the skillet, frying them until crispy, before adding the onions and garlic. Follow the remainder of the recipe as before, substituting 1 head of cauliflower, cut into florets, for the broccoli.

cheesy mushroom rice
Prepare the basic recipe, replacing the broccoli with 8 sliced medium mushrooms.

cheesy chicken & broccoli rice
Prepare the basic recipe, adding 9 ounces cooked, shredded chicken to the rice with the broccoli.

slow cooker pulled pork

Serve this pulled pork with fresh, buttered bread rolls to make pork sliders.

4 lb. pork shoulder

1 tbsp. olive oil

2 yellow onions, finely chopped

2 cloves garlic, finely chopped

3 cooking apples, peeled, cored and chopped

1/2 cup ketchup

1/4 cup apple cider vinegar

1/2 cup chicken broth

2 tsp. dried oregano

2 tbsp. whole-grain mustard

1/2 cup tomato paste

2 tbsp. brown sugar

Serves 6–8

Use a sharp knife to remove any skin and excess fat from the pork shoulder. Add the olive oil to a large skillet over a medium-high heat, and sear the pork shoulder until golden brown, turning until each side is done. Put it in a slow cooker on the high setting.

Drain the excess fat from the skillet and add the onions and garlic. Reduce the heat and sauté the onions and garlic until golden. Transfer to a saucepan, and add the apples, ketchup, apple cider vinegar, chicken broth, oregano, and mustard. Bring the mixture to a boil. Remove from the heat and pour into the slow cooker. Cook for 5 to 6 hours, or until the meat is falling apart and shreds easily.

Remove the meat from the slow cooker and let sit for 10 minutes. Pour the sauce into a saucepan and add the tomato paste and brown sugar. Bring to a boil, then simmer for 5 to 10 minutes, until reduced and thickened. Use two forks to pull and shred the pork and arrange it on a serving dish, pour 1/2 cup of the sauce over the meat and serve immediately with the remaining sauce on the side.

NOW TRY THIS

texas-style pulled pork
Replace the ketchup, dried oregano, and whole-grain mustard with 1 cup prepared barbecue sauce, 2 teaspoons dried thyme, and 1 tablespoon each prepared yellow mustard, Worcestershire sauce, and chili powder.

slow cooker pulled beef
Prepare the basic recipe, replacing the pork shoulder with 4 pounds beef chuck roast or brisket.

smoked pulled pork
Prepare the basic recipe, adding 2 tablespoons liquid smoke to the onions and garlic with the ketchup, apple cider vinegar, and chicken broth.

beef skewers with béarnaise sauce

This is a simple, traditional tapas dish, and it is a real crowd-pleaser. Grilled beef skewers dipped into a classic béarnaise sauce could please a stadium.

2 shallots, finely chopped

4 sprigs fresh tarragon

2/3 cup dry white wine

1/3 cup white wine vinegar

1/2 cup water

1 1/2 cups (3 sticks) unsalted butter

6 free-range egg yolks

1 lb. sirloin steak, cut into 3/4-in. (2-cm.) cubes

8 wooden skewers, soaked in water for 1 hour

2 tbsp. olive oil

sea salt and freshly ground black pepper

Serves 8

To make the béarnaise, mix the shallot, tarragon, wine, white wine vinegar, and water in a saucepan. Boil until reduced by two-thirds. Pour through a sieve, reserving all the juice and discarding the tarragon and shallot. Allow to cool slightly. Then, melt the butter in a pan over a low heat, until liquid. Turn up the heat and let the butter boil for 30 seconds. Pour the clear liquid into a measuring cup and discard the milky residue at the bottom of the pan. With a hand whisk, whisk the egg yolks and wine reduction together. Slowly, still whisking, add the butter in a thin, steady stream, until a medium-thick sauce has formed. Cover and set aside until the steak is cooked.

Meanwhile, heat a griddle pan or a barbecue grill until really hot and almost smoking. Thread the steak pieces equally among the wooden skewers. Drizzle with the olive oil, and sprinkle with salt and pepper. Lay the skewers on the griddle or grill and cook for 1 minute on each of the 4 sides. Serve the skewers piled up together on one big platter with a bowl of the béarnaise to dip into.

NOW TRY THIS

sesame beef skewers
Prepare the basic recipe, tossing the beef cubes in 1/4 cup sesame seeds before cooking.

herbed beef skewers
Prepare the basic recipe, tossing the beef cubes in 2 teaspoons fresh rosemary and 2 teaspoons fresh thyme before cooking.

venison skewers
Prepare the basic recipe, replacing the beef with venison fillet.

beef skewers with roasted garlic béarnaise sauce
Prepare the basic recipe, adding 2 heads puréed roasted garlic to the béarnaise.

spanish empanadas

You can find empanadas, bursting with local flavors, being served all over Latin America. They make a great dish for sharing.

2 tbsp. olive oil

2 medium onions, chopped

2 tsp. smoked sweet paprika

1/2 tsp. hot paprika

1/2 tsp. red chili flakes

1 tsp. ground cumin

1 tbsp. white vinegar

1 lb. lean ground beef

1 packet frozen puff pastry, thawed

1/4 cup raisins

4 oz. pitted green olives, chopped

1 large egg, lightly beaten

Makes 8

Preheat the oven to 350°F (175°C). Heat the oil in a large skillet, then add the chopped onions and sauté for 3 minutes, until they are translucent. Add both paprikas, the red chili flakes, cumin, and vinegar and stir until well combined. Add the ground beef and cook until the meat is browned. Drain half the fat from the skillet.

On a lightly floured surface, roll out the puff pastry 1/4-inch (6-mm) thick. Using a 5-inch (13-cm) cutter, cut out circles of pastry. One packet of puff pastry should yield 8 rounds. Using a pastry brush, glaze the top edge of each circle with water. Spoon 2 tablespoons of filling onto the lower half of the circle. Sprinkle each with the raisins and olives. Fold the top half of the circle over, pressing the edges to seal. Crimp the edge by twisting the pastry inward, from one side to the other. This will prevent the juices from leaking during baking. Glaze the tops of the empanadas with the egg. Prick the crust with a fork near the seam to allow steam to escape. Place the empanadas on a baking sheet lined with parchment paper, and bake for 25 minutes, or until the filling is hot and the crust is golden.

NOW TRY THIS

broccoli empanadas
Prepare the basic recipe, replacing the beef with 12 ounces cooked broccoli florets and 8 ounces ricotta cheese. Omit the raisins and olives.

chicken empanadas
Prepare the basic recipe, replacing the beef with 1 pound skinless chicken breast, cubed.

sausage empanadas
Prepare the basic recipe, replacing the beef with 1 pound mild Italian sausage, removed from its casing and crumbled.

spanish empanadas with hard-boiled egg
Prepare the basic recipe, adding 2 hard-boiled eggs, finely chopped, to the filling mixture with the raisins and olives.

spiced sausage bake

This is a hearty dish of spiced Italian sausage, pasta, tomato, and cheese.

1 tbsp. olive oil

1 lb. hot Italian sausage, casings removed

1 large yellow onion, chopped

1 clove garlic, finely chopped

2 large red bell peppers, seeded and chopped

1 hot red chile, finely chopped

1/2 cup tomato paste

1 (15 oz.) can crushed tomatoes

1 cup chicken broth

salt and freshly ground black pepper

4 1/2 cups short pasta; such as penne, spirals, or bows

4 oz. grated sharp cheddar cheese

4 oz. grated mozzarella

2 oz. grated Parmesan

1/2 cup chopped fresh basil

Serves 6–8

Preheat the oven to 375°F (190°C).

Place a large skillet over a medium-high heat and add the olive oil. Once the skillet is hot, add the sausage and cook until it has browned, stirring occasionally and using a spoon to break up any lumps. Drain off any excess fat.

Add the onion, garlic, peppers, and chile to the skillet and sauté until fragrant and lightly golden. Add the tomato paste, stir to combine, and then add the crushed tomatoes and chicken broth. Bring the sauce to a boil, reduce the heat and simmer for 15 to 20 minutes, until the sauce has thickened and reduced a little. Season with salt and pepper and remove from the heat. While the sauce is cooking, cook the pasta until just tender, drain, and then add it to the sauce. Mix well.

In a medium bowl, combine the cheeses and basil. Layer half of the pasta mixture into a deep 8 x 12-inch (20 x 30-cm) baking dish, top with half of the cheese mixture, then another layer of pasta and the remaining cheese. Bake for 20 to 30 minutes, until the cheese is melted, bubbling, and golden. Serve immediately.

NOW TRY THIS

sausage & bean bake
Prepare the basic recipe, omitting the chicken broth and replacing the pasta with 3 rinsed and drained 15-ounce cans mixed beans.

mild sausage bake
Prepare the basic recipe, omitting the chile and replacing the hot Italian sausage with 1 pound mild Italian sausage.

curried sausage bake
Omit the crushed tomatoes from the basic recipe. Add 1 tablespoon curry powder to the sausage with the onion and garlic. Follow the remainder of the recipe, adding 1 cup half-and-half to the sauce with the pasta.

chili

A spiced mix of ground beef and beans makes chili a wonderful dish to share at any potluck. Serve it straight from the pot with a ladle.

2 tbsp. olive oil

2 lb. ground beef

2 medium yellow onions, finely chopped

2 cloves garlic, finely chopped

1 tbsp. ground cumin

1 tsp. ground chili

1 tbsp. dried oregano

2 (15 oz.) cans kidney beans, rinsed and drained

1/2 cup tomato paste

2 (15 oz.) cans chopped tomatoes

1 cup beef broth

salt and freshly ground black pepper

Serves 6–8

Set a large pot over a medium-high heat and add the olive oil. Once hot, add the ground beef and cook, breaking up the large chunks with a spoon, until the beef is browned. Remove the beef from the pot and drain it on some paper towels.

Add the onions and garlic to the pot, reduce the heat to medium, and sauté until translucent and starting to color. Add the cumin, chili, and oregano, stir for a minute, then add the kidney beans, tomato paste, chopped tomatoes, and broth.

Return the ground beef to the pot and bring the chili to a boil. Reduce the heat to low and simmer gently for 1 1/2 to 2 hours, stirring occasionally to prevent sticking, until the chili is thick and rich. Season with salt and freshly ground pepper and serve hot.

NOW TRY THIS

turkey chili
Prepare the basic recipe, replacing the ground beef with 2 pounds ground turkey.

vegetarian chili
Omit the ground beef and beef broth. Instead, sauté the onions and garlic in the olive oil, add the cumin, chili, and oregano then add two 15-ounce cans of rinsed and drained black beans along with the kidney beans. Complete the recipe as directed, replacing the beef broth with vegetable broth or water.

macaroni with meatballs

Serving meatballs with a short pasta like rigatoni or macaroni, rather than more traditional spaghetti, is easier to serve and eat at potluck parties.

1 onion, peeled and chopped

1/2 cup olive oil

1 lb. ground pork

2 eggs, beaten

salt and freshly ground black pepper

1 clove garlic, peeled and finely chopped

handful of fresh flat-leaf parsley, chopped

5 or 6 tbsp. fine, dry bread crumbs

3 cups passata (puréed tomatoes)

handful of mixed fresh herbs, finely chopped

3 1/3 cups large macaroni

Serves 6

Fry the onion in the olive oil until softened but not browned, then take off the heat until required. Mix the pork with the eggs, seasoning, garlic, parsley, and 2 to 3 tablespoons of the bread crumbs. Using wet hands to prevent sticking, shape the mixture into meatballs about the size of large olives. Roll the meatballs in the remaining bread crumbs and fry gently in the reheated onion and oil for about 2 minutes, or until sealed and lightly browned. Drain off any excess oil and add the passata and the chopped mixed herbs. Simmer together for about an hour, stirring frequently and adding a little water if necessary.

Bring a large saucepan of salted water to a boil. Put the macaroni into the water and stir thoroughly. Replace the lid and return to a boil. Remove or adjust the lid once the water is boiling again. Cook according to the package instructions until al dente. Drain, and return to the pot. Pour over the sauce and the meatballs, mix gently, and serve immediately.

NOW TRY THIS

macaroni with pork & prosciutto meatballs
For extra flavor, add 3 or 4 slices of finely chopped prosciutto to the minced pork, and then proceed as in the main recipe.

macaroni with garlicky meatballs
If you love garlic, add a clove or two, finely minced, to the minced pork mixture, then proceed as in the main recipe.

macaroni with spicy meatballs
Add 1 teaspoon ground chili to the pork mixture, and then proceed as in the main recipe.

thai fish cakes

These spicy and flavorful little fish cakes are wonderful as a starter or as a main course. Serve with soy sauce for dipping.

1 tsp. canola oil, for greasing

1 lb. 2 oz. white fish fillet

1 egg, lightly beaten

2 tbsp. cornstarch

1 tbsp. fish sauce

1–2 tsp. red Thai curry paste, or to taste

1 tsp. seeded and finely chopped red chile

2 tbsp. freshly chopped cilantro

salt and freshly ground black pepper

2 scallions, chopped

soy sauce, to serve

Makes 8–9

Lightly brush a baking sheet with canola oil. Chop the fish into 1/2-inch (1.25-cm) pieces, and put it in a food processor. Pulse until coarsely chopped. Add the egg, cornstarch, fish sauce, curry paste, chile, and cilantro, and season with salt and pepper. Pulse until combined. Mix in the scallions. Using your hands, form the mixture into small fish cakes about 3 inches (7.5cm) in diameter.

Preheat the oven to 440°F (225°C). Put the fish cakes on the oiled baking sheet, set it on the high rack of the oven, and cook for 5 minutes per side, or until lightly browned and cooked through. Serve with soy sauce.

You can make your own red Thai curry paste by processing 2 shallots, 2 cloves garlic, 2 red chiles, 1-inch (2.5-cm) piece fresh gingerroot, 1 tablespoon fish or soy sauce, 1 teaspoon each ground coriander and cumin, 1 chopped lemongrass stalk, zest and juice of 1 lime, and salt and pepper. Cover and store any surplus in the refrigerator for up to 1 week, or freeze for up to 1 month.

NOW TRY THIS

thai salmon & spinach fish cakes
Replace the white fish with two skinless smoked salmon fillets. Steam 1 cup spinach for a few minutes, until wilted, and stir into the mixture after the scallions.

thai tuna fish cakes
Replace the white fish fillet with two 5-ounce cans tuna. Drain and add to the food processor with the other ingredients.

cheesy chicken bake

This rich and flavorful dish can be prepared a day ahead of time, up to the point of baking. Simply cover it and refrigerate until you are ready to cook.

1 tsp. sunflower oil, for greasing
8 oz. cream cheese, softened
1 cup chicken broth
2 tbsp. chopped fresh rosemary
1 clove garlic, crushed
salt and freshly ground black pepper
8 medium potatoes, peeled and chopped into 1-in. (2.5-cm.) pieces
2 lb. skinless chicken thighs, quartered
4 oz. grated sharp cheddar cheese
2 oz. grated Parmesan

Serves 6–8

Preheat the oven to 350°F (175°C) and lightly grease a 7 x 10-inch (18 x 25-cm) baking dish with sunflower oil.

In a large bowl, beat together the cream cheese and chicken broth until combined. Stir in the rosemary and garlic and season with salt and pepper. Add the potato and chicken pieces to the cream cheese mixture, along with half of the cheddar cheese, and toss gently to coat.

Put the chicken, potato, and cream cheese mixture in the prepared baking dish, and sprinkle the Parmesan and remaining cheddar cheese over the top. Bake for 1 hour, until the chicken and potatoes are tender and cooked, increasing the heat to 400°F (200°C) for the last 10 minutes to brown the top. Serve immediately.

NOW TRY THIS

mexican chicken bake
Prepare the basic recipe, replacing the cream cheese with 1 cup hot tomato salsa and the rosemary with 1/4 cup chopped fresh cilantro. Add 1/2 cup sliced black olives with the potato and chicken pieces.

cheesy turkey bake
Prepare the basic recipe, replacing the chicken with 2 pounds turkey steak cut into bite-size pieces.

cheesy ham bake
Prepare the basic recipe, replacing the chicken with 12 ounces shredded smoked ham.

sides

The perfect complement to any party food, sides
needn't be an afterthought. The following dishes will
have guests coming back for more.

scalloped potatoes & ham

The perfect combination of ham, potatoes, and cheese makes this dish an old favorite. It can be assembled the day before you need it, and then refrigerated until it's time to bake and serve.

1 cup heavy cream
1 cup milk
10 oz. finely diced ham
4 oz. grated sharp cheddar cheese
salt and freshly ground black pepper
8 medium potatoes, peeled and cut into 1/4-in. (6-mm.) slices
1 medium yellow onion, cut into 1/4-in. (6-mm.) slices
Serves 6–8

Preheat the oven to 350°F (175°C) and lightly grease a deep 7 x 10-inch (18 x 25-cm) baking pan with butter.

In a mixing bowl, beat together the cream and milk until well blended, and then stir in the ham and cheese and season with salt and pepper.

Add the sliced potatoes and onions to the cream mixture and toss them gently to coat. Pour the mixture into the prepared pan, spreading it out evenly, and bake for 1 to 1 1/2 hours, until the potatoes are cooked through and the top is golden. Serve immediately.

NOW TRY THIS

cheesy scalloped sweet potato
Prepare the basic recipe, replacing the potatoes with 4 medium sweet potatoes.

scalloped potatoes & bacon
Prepare the basic recipe, replacing the ham with 8 strips of bacon, coarsely chopped and cooked until crispy.

scalloped potatoes & scallions
Prepare the basic recipe, replacing the yellow onion with 4 finely sliced scallions.

grilled vegetable platter

The colors of the vegetables piled high on this platter will look spectacular.

1 lb. thick asparagus spears

2 zucchini

1 bunch carrots (about 8 oz.), peeled

1 red bell pepper

1 yellow bell pepper

1 large red onion, peeled

2 tbsp. vegetable oil

1 tbsp. fresh thyme

salt and freshly ground black pepper

for the glaze

1/2 cup balsamic vinegar

1/4 cup maple syrup

Serves 6

Trim the woody ends of the asparagus spears. Cut the zucchini and carrots lengthwise into thirds. Seed and core the red and yellow peppers; cut each into eighths. Set the onion on its root end and cut it into 8 wedges, leaving the end intact. Place the vegetables in a bowl. Toss the vegetables with the oil, thyme, salt, and pepper.

Place the vegetables on a grill preheated to medium. Cook for 3 minutes. Remove the asparagus and keep warm. Rotate the remaining vegetables 90 degrees to make crosshatched grill marks. Continue cooking, rotating every 3 minutes, until tender-crisp. Remove from the heat.

Meanwhile, in a small saucepan, bring the vinegar and maple syrup to a boil. Boil for about 2 minutes, until thickened. Brush one-quarter of the glaze over the vegetables. Turn over and brush again. Transfer to a serving platter and brush with the remaining glaze.

NOW TRY THIS

with basil aïoli
Omit the glaze. Make a dressing of basil aïoli by whisking together 1 tablespoon torn basil leaves, 2 large cloves garlic, crushed, 1 egg yolk, 2 teaspoons fresh lemon juice, and 1/2 cup olive oil. Add the oil gradually in a thin stream, not all at once. Put the aïoli in a bowl to serve with the vegetables.

with fresh basil vinaigrette
Omit the glaze. Make a vinaigrette dressing by whisking together 1 cup extra-virgin olive oil, 1/4 cup fresh lemon juice, 1 tablespoon chopped fresh basil, 2 crushed cloves garlic, and 1 tablespoon Dijon mustard. Use to dress the vegetables just before serving.

herby couscous

Nothing could be simpler or easier than cooking couscous. Serve hot with broiled meat, chicken, fish, or stew, or cold as a salad. If serving cold, add the scallions and herbs once the couscous has cooled.

2 1/2 cups couscous

1 vegetable or chicken bouillon cube

7 cups boiling water

2/3 cup mixed seeds

4 scallions, sliced

2/3 cup chopped fresh mint, parsley, and/or cilantro

3 tbsp. olive oil

juice of 1 lemon

Serves 8

Put the couscous in a heatproof bowl. Dissolve the bouillon cube in the boiling water. Pour the bouillon over the couscous and stir well. Cover the bowl with a damp kitchen towel and leave for 5 minutes. The couscous should be soft. Fluff it with a fork.

Meanwhile, toast the mixed seeds in a small skillet until just beginning to brown.

Toss into the couscous with the scallion, herbs, olive oil, and lemon juice and serve hot or warm.

NOW TRY THIS

couscous with tomatoes
Add 4 medium skinned, seeded, and chopped tomatoes after the couscous has cooled. Omit the seeds.

spicy couscous & garbanzo beans
Add two-thirds 14-ounce can garbanzo beans (1 cup), drained, to the uncooked couscous. Stir in 1 teaspoon harissa with the bouillon.

tabbouleh
Replace the couscous with bulgur wheat and allow to stand for 1 hour. Add all the other ingredients except the seeds. Also add 2 large chopped tomatoes (preferably seeded and skinned) and 8 inches (20 cm) chopped cucumber.

cheesy turkey & enchilada bake

This dish of layered tortillas, meat, salsa, and cheese, baked until golden, is like a Mexican-style lasagna. Equally delicious on its own or with sour cream and salad, make it as spicy as you like by using hot, medium, or mild tomato salsa.

6 (10-in./25-cm.) wheat tortillas
2 cups tomato salsa
13 1/2 oz. cooked, shredded turkey
2 cups frozen corn kernels, thawed
1/4 cup chopped fresh cilantro
4 oz. grated sharp cheddar cheese
4 oz. grated mozzarella cheese

Serves 6–8

Preheat the oven to 375°F (190°C) and lightly grease a deep 7 x 10-inch (18 x 25-cm) baking pan with butter.

Put two of the tortillas into the baking pan, overlapping them slightly, so that they cover the base. Spread them evenly with one-third of the salsa. Distribute half of the turkey over the salsa, along with half of the corn, half of the cilantro, and one-third each of the cheddar and mozzarella cheeses.

Place two more of the tortillas on top, and layer them with half of the remaining salsa, and all of the remaining turkey, corn, and cilantro. Top this with half of the remaining cheeses.

Place the final two tortillas on top and spread them with the remaining salsa and cheeses. Bake for 30 to 40 minutes, until heated through and golden and bubbling on top. Serve immediately.

NOW TRY THIS

cheesy pork & enchilada bake
Prepare the basic recipe, replacing the cooked turkey with 15 ounces cooked pulled or shredded pork.

refried bean & enchilada bake
Prepare the basic recipe, replacing the cooked turkey with one 16-ounce can refried beans.

cheesy chicken & enchilada bake
Prepare the basic recipe, replacing the cooked turkey with 13 1/2 ounces cooked shredded chicken.

garlic bread

This is a classic side dish that is ever popular; buttery, hot, garlicky bread. Here it is made using a baguette, but it is equally delicious made with other types of bread.

1 large baguette
2 cloves garlic, finely chopped
2/3 cup (1 1/4 sticks) butter, softened
1/4 cup chopped fresh parsley
1/4 tsp. salt
1/4 tsp. freshly ground black pepper

Serves 6–8

Preheat the oven to 400°F (200°C). Use a serrated knife to slice the baguette in half crossways, and each half into 1-inch (2.5-cm) slices crossways, stopping just before the bottom so the slices stay connected.

Put the garlic, butter, parsley, and salt and pepper in a small mixing bowl and mix with a fork until well combined.

Butter each slice of the baguette with the garlic butter, taking care to keep the loaf joined. Once each slice has been buttered, wrap the loaf in aluminum foil. Bake for 5 to 10 minutes, until the bread is hot and the butter has melted. Uncover the bread for the last few minutes if you want a crispier crust, and serve immediately.

NOW TRY THIS

garlic & herb bread
Prepare the basic recipe, adding 1 tablespoon chopped fresh thyme and 1 tablespoon chopped fresh oregano to the garlic, along with the butter and parsley.

cheesy garlic bread
Prepare the basic recipe, and after buttering the bread with the garlic butter, distribute 4 ounces grated sharp cheddar cheese between the slices of bread. Continue as directed, baking until the cheese is melted.

garlic & mustard bread
Prepare the basic recipe, adding 1 tablespoon whole-grain mustard and 2 tablespoons grated Parmesan to the garlic with the butter and parsley.

patatas bravas

Patatas bravas simply translates as "fierce" potatoes. They are sliced fried potatoes smothered in a rich tomato sauce with a hint of smoky spiciness.

1 lb. waxy potatoes (such as Yukon Gold), well scrubbed

2 cups mild olive oil

for the tomato sauce

3 tbsp. olive oil

1 small onion, finely chopped

1 clove garlic, finely chopped

1 small dried red chile, finely chopped

1/2 tsp. smoked paprika

4 large ripe plum tomatoes, chopped

2 tsp. tomato paste

salt and freshly ground black pepper

fresh flat-leaf parsley, to garnish (optional)

Serves 6

Cut the potatoes into even-sized chunks. Add them to a large pan half-filled with the oil and heat gently over a low flame until small bubbles rise to the surface. Cook the potatoes like this — almost poaching them in the oil — for 12 to 15 minutes, until they are just tender. Then, increase the heat and deep-fry the potato pieces until golden brown.

While the potatoes are cooking, prepare the sauce. Heat the oil in a small saucepan. Fry the onion, garlic, and chile in the hot oil for 3 to 4 minutes, until softened but not colored. Stir in the paprika and cook for a few seconds more. Add the tomatoes to the pan. Stir in the tomato paste and 1/2 cup water. Cook over low heat for about 10 minutes until the tomatoes are well softened, stirring occasionally. Season to taste with salt and pepper. Lift the potatoes out of the oil with a slotted spoon and drain on paper towels. Put into a warmed dish, add the tomato sauce, garnish with parsley (if desired), and serve.

NOW TRY THIS

patatas bravas with piquillo peppers
Add 2 chopped piquillo peppers (jarred, roasted red peppers) to the sauce at the end of cooking.

patatas bravas with chorizo
Add slices of fried chorizo on top of the dish.

patatas bravas with blood sausage
Add 1 Spanish blood sausage, chopped and fried, to the cooked potatoes just before covering with the sauce.

garlic spinach with pine nuts

This is another classic tapas dish that works well as party food. It is delicious served with crusty bread.

1/3 cup olive oil
1/2 cup pine nuts
4 garlic cloves, crushed
1 lb. 2 oz. fresh spinach
salt and ground black pepper

Serves 8

Heat the oil in a large non-stick saucepan and cook the pine nuts for 2 to 3 minutes, until golden. Add the garlic and cook gently for about 30 seconds.

Add the spinach and cook, tossing the leaves, for about 3 minutes, until wilted. Season with salt and pepper and serve.

NOW TRY THIS

garlic spinach with pine nuts & raisins
Prepare the basic recipe, adding 4 tablespoons raisins before serving.

garlic spinach with pine nuts & chorizo
Prepare the basic recipe, cooking 4 ounces chopped chorizo with the pine nuts.

garlic spinach with pine nuts & chili
Prepare the basic recipe, adding a good couple of pinches of dried chili flakes with the spinach.

lemon & garlic spinach with pine nuts
Prepare the basic recipe, adding a good couple of squeezes of lemon juice with the seasoning.

feta & olive stuffed mushrooms

Stuffed mushrooms can be filled with a variety of flavors, and are a simple and impressive dish to take to a potluck. These can be prepared a day ahead, covered, and refrigerated, and then baked when needed.

sunflower oil, for greasing

12 medium mushrooms, cleaned and the stalks discarded

for the filling

24 pitted olives, finely chopped

4 oz. crumbled feta cheese

2 oz. grated mozzarella

1/4 cup chopped fresh parsley

freshly ground black pepper

Makes 12

Preheat the oven to 375°F (190°C) and lightly grease a baking sheet with sunflower oil. Put the mushrooms on the baking sheet upside down, so they resemble cups.

Combine the olives, feta, mozzarella, and half of the chopped parsley in a mixing bowl. Mix until combined and season with freshly ground black pepper.

Divide the filling evenly between the mushroom cups, pressing it down gently. Bake for 20 to 25 minutes, until they are cooked and golden. Put them on a serving tray and sprinkle with the remaining parsley. Serve immediately.

NOW TRY THIS

bacon & parmesan stuffed mushrooms
For the filling, mix 6 strips of finely chopped, fried bacon, 1 ounce grated Parmesan, 2 finely chopped scallions, 1/4 cup bread crumbs and 2 ounces mozzarella. Top with grated Parmesan.

cheese & bell pepper stuffed mushrooms
For the filling, mix 4 ounces roasted, chopped red bell pepper, 2 ounces grated sharp cheddar cheese, 2 ounces shredded mozzarella and 2 tablespoons chopped fresh oregano.

pesto & tomato stuffed mushrooms
For the filling, mix 3 medium diced tomatoes, 1/4 cup basil pesto, 2 ounces grated mozzarella and 2 tablespoons chopped fresh basil.

spiced potato wedges

These are always delicious served as an accompaniment. Cumin and paprika work brilliantly together, but other spice combinations — such as creole spice mix, jerk spice mix, or curry powder — are also excellent. For vegans, serve with plain soy yogurt.

2/3 cup olive oil
1 tsp. paprika
1 tsp. ground cumin
salt and pepper
8 large baking potatoes
2 cups sour cream, to serve
snipped fresh chives (optional)
Serves 8

Preheat the oven to 400°F (200°C).

In a large bowl, mix the oil with the paprika, cumin, and a little salt and pepper. Cut each potato into eight wedges and toss in the spiced oil to coat.

Spread the coated wedges onto a baking sheet and bake for 25 to 30 minutes, turning once, until evenly crisp and browned. Serve with a side of sour cream and garnished with snipped chives, if available.

NOW TRY THIS

spiced sweet potato wedges
Replace the potatoes with sweet potatoes.

parmesan-loaded potato wedges
Omit the cumin and add 2/3 cup grated Parmesan cheese to the spice mixture. Cook as directed. When cooked, toss in another 2/3 cup grated Parmesan mixed with 1/4 cup chopped parsley.

lemon & thyme potato wedges
Replace the cumin with the juice of 4 lemons and 4 teaspoons dried thyme.

crispy potato wedges
Replace the paprika and cumin with salt flakes or roughly ground sea salt. Serve with mayonnaise or sour cream, if desired.

desserts

Every potluck needs some impressive treats to finish the meal. Decadent, scrumptious, delightful, and refreshing, it's all here and easily prepared ahead of time, allowing you to enjoy the party.

chocolate freezer cake

This cake is so simple (no cooking is required) and so delicious. Prepare it up to a week in advance and keep it covered in the freezer.

3 cups whipping cream

3/4 cup condensed milk

1/4 cup drinking chocolate powder

1 tsp. vanilla extract

6 oz. milk chocolate chips

15 chocolate cookies (about 7 oz.)

2 oz. dark chocolate, grated or shaved into curls with a peeler, to serve

Serves 8–10

Line the base and sides of a 7-inch- (18-cm-) square cake pan with plastic wrap, making sure it overhangs the edges of the pan.

Combine the cream, condensed milk, chocolate powder, and vanilla extract in a mixing bowl and use an electric mixer to beat until soft peaks form. Gently fold in the chocolate chips.

Spoon one-quarter of the cream mixture into the prepared pan, smoothing it out with the back of the spoon. Add a single layer of the cookies, leaving a 1/2-inch (1.25-cm) border between them and the edges of the pan. Repeat this process for two more layers, then cover with the remaining cream mixture.

Put the cake pan in the freezer for at least 8 hours, or overnight, until frozen. To serve, remove the cake from the freezer and allow it to sit at room temperature for 20 minutes to soften slightly.

Remove the cake from the pan by gently pulling the overhanging plastic wrap to ease it out. Put it on a serving plate and sprinkle it with the grated dark chocolate. Cut into pieces and serve.

NOW TRY THIS

cookies & cream freezer cake
Omit the chocolate powder and replace the chocolate cookies with 18 Oreo cookies.

funfetti freezer cake
Omit the chocolate powder and grated chocolate. Replace the chocolate chips with 1/2 cup rainbow sprinkles and the cookies with 14 graham crackers. Garnish with 1/4 cup rainbow sprinkles.

chocolate & cherry freezer cake
Prepare the basic recipe, dividing one (14 1/2 ounce) can of drained, pitted cherries evenly between each layer. Garnish with fresh cherries when serving.

chocolate & caramel freezer cake
Prepare the basic recipe, drizzling 1/4 cup of caramel sauce over each cookie layer. Drizzle with extra caramel sauce when serving.

cherry pavlova bites

Crispy on the outside and gooey on the inside, these mini pavlovas just melt in the mouth.

6 egg whites, at room temperature

1 1/4 cups superfine sugar

1 tsp. lemon juice

2 tsp. cornstarch

8 oz. mascarpone

8 oz. crème fraîche

1 tbsp. confectioners' sugar

1 tsp. vanilla extract

8 tbsp. good-quality black cherry preserve

Makes 25

Preheat the oven to 250°F (120°C), and line two large baking sheets with parchment. In a clean bowl, using an electric mixer, whisk the egg whites until they form soft peaks. Add the sugar a tablespoon at a time, whisking, until it has all been incorporated. Whisk in the lemon juice, and fold in the cornstarch.

Drop tablespoons of meringue onto the lined baking sheets. Using the back of a teaspoon, form them into rounds, with a shallow indentation in the middle. Bake for 45 to 50 minutes, until just firm to the touch, swapping the trays around halfway through cooking time. Turn the oven off, and leave the pavlovas to dry out in the oven, until they are cold.

Mix together the mascarpone, crème fraîche, confectioners' sugar, and vanilla extract. Put 1/2 teaspoon cherry preserve into the middle of each pavlova, followed by 1 tablespoon mascarpone mixture, and another teaspoon cherry preserve. Swirl together with a toothpick. The unfilled pavlovas will keep for 2 days in an airtight container. Fill an hour before serving.

NOW TRY THIS

blueberry & lemon cream pavlova bites
Omit the cherry preserve. Top the pavlovas with the mascarpone mix, and add 1 teaspoon lemon curd and a few blueberries.

mont blanc pavlova bites
Prepare the basic recipe, omitting the cherry preserve, and substituting sweetened chestnut purée. Dust with confectioners' sugar to serve.

chocolate pavlova bites with caramel sauce
Prepare the basic recipe, adding 2 tablespoons sifted unsweetened cocoa powder to the beaten egg whites halfway through whisking. Omit the cherry preserve, top with the mascarpone mix, and drizzle each pavlova with caramel topping before serving, as before.

blueberry crumble bars

You can make these sweet and fruity bars a day or two before you need them, which makes them a perfect easy treat for a potluck party.

3 cups all-purpose flour
1 cup superfine sugar
1 tsp. baking powder
1/4 tsp. salt
zest and juice of 1 lemon
8 oz. cold butter
1 egg, lightly beaten
1/2 cup sugar
4 tsp. cornstarch
1 lb. fresh blueberries
Makes about 16

Preheat the oven to 375°F (190°C), and grease a 9 x 13-inch (23 x 33-cm) shallow baking pan.

In a large bowl, whisk together the flour, sugar, and baking powder. Add the salt and lemon zest. Cut the cold butter into small pieces, add to the flour mixture and, using either your fingers or a pastry cutter, mix until the mixture resembles fine bread crumbs. Stir in the egg, until the mixture is crumbly. Put half the mixture into the pan and gently pat down.

In a medium bowl, stir together the lemon juice, sugar, and cornstarch. Add the blueberries, and gently stir until they are well coated. Spread over the dough in the pan, and sprinkle the remaining dough over the top. Place the pan in the oven, and bake for 50 to 55 minutes or until the top is lightly browned. Leave to cool in the pan completely, before cutting into squares. Store somewhere cool, in an airtight container until required.

NOW TRY THIS

apple & raspberry bars
Replace the blueberries with 3 small red apples, peeled, cored, and chopped, mixed with 9 ounces raspberries.

chocolate & caramel oat bars
Replace 3/4 of the flour with 1/2 cup rolled oats. Gently press the mixture into the pan and bake for 20 minutes. Omit the blueberries.

Melt 48 soft caramels with 1/2 cup heavy cream. Sprinkle the base with semisweet chocolate chips and drizzle the caramel over the top. Sprinkle the remaining dough over the top and bake for 25 minutes.

cherry pie bars
Replace the blueberries with 4 cups pitted fresh cherries. Bake as before.

turtle pie

A decadent twist on that classic dessert, this pie combines a soft, creamy filling with caramel, chocolate, and pecans.

34 (about 10 oz.) Oreo cookies, crushed
1/4 cup (1/2 stick) butter, melted
for the filling
8 oz. cream cheese, softened
1/2 cup confectioners' sugar
1 1/2 cups whipping cream
5 oz. caramel pieces
for the topping
2 oz. chopped pecans
2 oz. milk chocolate, grated or shaved into curls with a peeler
1/4 cup caramel sauce
Serves 8–10

Line an 8-inch (20-cm) pie pan with plastic wrap, making sure the edges of the plastic wrap overhang the sides of the pan to help to remove the pie. Put the cookies and butter into a mixing bowl and mix until well combined. Press the mixture into the bottom and sides of the pie pan and refrigerate while you prepare the filling.

Put the cream cheese and confectioners' sugar in a large mixing bowl and use an electric beater on medium speed to beat them together until they are well combined. Add the cream and continue to mix on medium speed until it is incorporated. Scrape down the sides of the bowl and gradually increase the speed to high. Beat the mixture for a few minutes, until it is thick and fluffy.

Fold the caramel pieces through the cream cheese mixture and then pour it into the prepared crust, smoothing the top with the back of a spoon. Return the pie to the refrigerator to set overnight.

To serve, pull the edges of the plastic to release the pie from the pan. Set it on a serving plate, sprinkle the pecans and chocolate over the top and drizzle with caramel sauce. Serve immediately.

NOW TRY THIS

snickers pie
Prepare the basic recipe, replacing the pecans with 2 1/2 ounces chopped, roasted peanuts.

salted caramel pie
Prepare the basic recipe, omitting the pecans. Increase the caramel sauce for the topping to 1/2 cup. Sprinkle 1/4 to 1/2 teaspoon kosher salt over the top of the caramel sauce.

chocolate peanut butter pie
Prepare the basic recipe, omitting the caramel pieces, pecans, and caramel sauce. Swirl 1/2 cup peanut butter through the filling and decorate the top of the pie with 2 1/2 ounces chopped, roasted peanuts and 1/4 cup chocolate sauce.

chocolate french fancies

These little tarts have a delicious, sweet chocolate pastry.

4 oz. butter, cold from the fridge and cubed (plus a little extra for greasing)

2 3/4 cups all-purpose flour

1/4 cup unsweetened cocoa powder, sifted

2 oz. shortening, cold from the fridge and cubed

1/4 tsp. salt

3 tbsp. superfine sugar

6 oz. semisweet chocolate

2 oz. milk chocolate

2/3 cup whipping cream

1 tsp. vanilla extract

2 oz. butter (additional to above)

1 egg yolk

1/2 cup caramel

1 cup heavy cream

2 tbsp. confectioners' sugar

Makes 48

Lightly grease 48 mini-muffin pan cups with a little butter. In a food processor, pulse the flour, cocoa, 4 ounces of cold butter, shortening, and salt, until the mixture resembles coarse bread crumbs. Add the sugar and pulse again briefly.

Add 5 tablespoons ice-cold water, pulse, add another tablespoon and pulse again until a dough comes together, adding extra water if necessary. Turn the dough out onto a lightly floured worktop, and knead into a round. Roll out to just under 1/8 inches (3 mm) thick, and cut out rounds with a 2 1/4-inch (6-cm) plain cutter. Line the pan cups with the pastry, then chill for 30 minutes.

Preheat the oven to 400°F (200°C). Place a few baking beans in each pastry case, and bake for 15 minutes. Remove from the oven, take out the baking beans and transfer the pastry shells to a wire rack to cool. Gently heat both chocolates, the whipping cream, and the vanilla until the chocolate has melted. Beat in 2 ounces butter a little at a time. Beat in the egg yolk, then remove from the heat and let cool. Put 1/2 teaspoon of caramel in the bottom of each pastry case. Add 1 teaspoon of the chocolate mixture to each, and smooth the top. Whisk the heavy cream and confectioners' sugar until it forms soft peaks, and pipe swirls on top of the tarts.

NOW TRY THIS

chocolate-orange french fancies
Prepare the basic recipe. Substitute a little orange marmalade for the caramel, and orange-flavored chocolate for the semisweet and milk chocolates. Cook and serve as before.

chocolate & apricot french fancies
Prepare the basic recipe, substituting apricot jam for the caramel. Cook and serve as before.

chocolate & peanut butter french fancies
Prepare the basic recipe, substituting peanut butter for the caramel. Cook and serve as before.

chocolate & raspberry french fancies
Prepare the basic recipe, substituting raspberry jam for the caramel. Cook and serve as before.

chocolate chip cookie dough dip

This dip is wonderful with graham crackers, strawberries on sticks, or fresh fruit cut into slices. It tastes as good as chocolate chip cookie dough about to be baked in the oven.

8 oz. full fat cream cheese

1/2 cup (1 stick) butter

1 cup confectioners' sugar, sifted

1/4 cup brown sugar

1 1/2 tsp. vanilla paste or extract

3/4 cup semisweet chocolate chips

3/4 cup toffee bits

Serves 4–6

In the bowl of a food processor, pulse together the cream cheese and butter, until smooth. Add both sugars and the vanilla paste, and pulse again to combine.

Transfer the mixture to a medium bowl, add the chocolate chips and toffee bits, and mix until combined. Store covered in the refrigerator until required, and serve with graham crackers, pretzels, or fresh strawberries on sticks, for dipping.

NOW TRY THIS

pumpkin & chocolate chip cookie dough
Omit the toffee bits, add 1/2 cup pumpkin purée, and double the amounts of confectioners' sugar and brown sugar.

double chocolate mint cookie dough
Replace the toffee bits and with mint chocolate chips. Add 1/4 cup milk chocolate chips to the recipe.

peanut butter & chocolate cookie dough
Replace the toffee bits with 8 ounces peanut butter cup minis. Cut the amount of confectioners' sugar to 1/2 cup and add an extra 1/4 cup brown sugar and 1/4 cup creamy peanut butter to the recipe.

caramel & pretzel magic bars

As the name implies, these bars are magic! Simply layer the ingredients in the pan, bake and voila! A scrumptious, chewy, crunchy treat that is great for sharing.

14 graham crackers, crushed (about 7 oz.)

6 tbsp. melted butter

for the topping

2 oz. sweetened coconut flakes

6 oz. chocolate chips

3 oz. chopped walnuts

3 oz. mini pretzels

1 cup sweetened condensed milk

1/2 cup caramel sauce

Serves 8–10

Preheat the oven to 375°F (190°C) and line an 8-inch- (20-cm-) square baking pan with baking parchment. Combine the graham crackers and melted butter in a mixing bowl and mix well. Press the mixture into the bottom of the prepared pan.

Sprinkle the coconut flakes, chocolate chips, and walnuts evenly over the crust, followed by the pretzels. Drizzle the condensed milk evenly over the topping ingredients, followed by the caramel sauce. Bake for 25 to 35 minutes, until bubbling and golden.

Remove from the oven and let cool in the pan until warm. Remove from the pan and cut into bars while still warm. Let cool completely before serving.

NOW TRY THIS

chocolate & pecan magic bars
Prepare the basic recipe, omitting the walnuts, pretzels, and caramel sauce. Increase the chocolate chips to 9 ounces and replace the walnuts with 4 ounces chopped pecans.

popcorn & caramel magic bars
Prepare the basic recipe, omitting the walnuts replacing the pretzels with 2 ounces popped popcorn.

peanut butter cup magic bars
Prepare the basic recipe, omitting the pretzels. Replace the chocolate chips with 9 ounces chopped peanut butter cups and the walnuts with 5 ounces roasted peanuts.

passion cake & cookie sandwiches

These delicious cookies taste like a little bite of heaven.

2 cups all-purpose flour
1 tsp. baking powder
1 tsp. baking soda
1 tsp. ground cinnamon
1 tsp. pumpkin pie spice
1/2 tsp. ground nutmeg
1/4 tsp. salt
1 cup (2 sticks) butter, at room temperature
1 cup superfine sugar
1 cup packed light brown sugar
2 eggs, at room temperature
1 tsp. vanilla extract
2 cups rolled oats
8 oz. finely grated carrots
1/4 cup finely chopped walnuts
8 oz. cream cheese

Makes 40 cookie sandwiches

In a large bowl, sift the flour, baking powder, baking soda, cinnamon, pumpkin pie spice, nutmeg, and salt. In a separate mixing bowl, beat the butter with the sugars until light and fluffy. Add the eggs, one at a time, beating well between each one, then add the vanilla and beat until combined. Stir in the flour mixture, and mix in the oats, carrots, and walnuts. Chill in the refrigerator for 2 hours.

Line 2 baking sheets with parchment. Preheat the oven to 350°F (175°C). Form the dough into about 40 small balls on the baking sheets, 2 inches (5 cm) apart, and bake for 12 to 15 minutes, until lightly browned and a little crisp on the edges. Cool on wire racks.

Once cooled completely, spread the cream cheese on half the cookies, and sandwich together with the remaining cookies. Store in an airtight container for 2 to 3 days in the refrigerator, and bring to room temperature before eating.

NOW TRY THIS

passion & ginger cookie sandwiches
Replace the pumpkin pie spice with 1 teaspoon ground ginger. Finely chop 1/2 ounce candied ginger and add it to the cream cheese filling.

passion & cardamom cookie sandwiches
Add the crushed seeds of 6 cardamom pods to the cookie dough mixture.

passion & coffee cake cookie sandwiches
Omit the pumpkin pie spice. Add 2 teaspoons instant coffee powder, mixed with 1 tablespoon hot water, to the cream cheese filling.

tropical passion cake cookie sandwiches
Replace the rolled oats with 1/3 cup flaked coconut and the walnuts with chopped macadamia nuts.

moroccan orange & date salad

This is a refreshing fruit salad that brings the flavors of Morocco to your table. The oranges are served in a simple syrup that can be adapted and used for other fruits, making this a versatile recipe, too.

syrup
1 1/4 cups white sugar
1/4 cup lemon juice
1 cup water
1 tsp. ground cinnamon

salad
1/3 cup slivered almonds
8–12 medium oranges, peeled and sliced
2 cups chopped pitted dates

Serves 8

Combine the syrup ingredients in a medium-sized saucepan. Bring to a boil, stirring, until the sugar has dissolved. Let cool.

Meanwhile, heat a medium-sized skillet and toast the almonds, stirring frequently, until lightly golden. Set aside to cool.

Put the orange slices in a bowl and pour over the cooled syrup. Add the dates, then leave to stand for about 30 minutes to infuse. Sprinkle over the toasted almonds to serve.

NOW TRY THIS

quick orange & date salad
Omit the syrup. Pour 1 cup orange and mango juice over the fruit and sprinkle with ground cinnamon.

spiced orange, date & pomegranate salad
Add the seeds of 1 small pomegranate with the dates.

spiced peaches & dates
Replace the oranges with 8 large peaches, peeled, pitted, and sliced.

minted oranges & strawberries
Add 32 sliced strawberries to the oranges and use 1/4 cup chopped fresh mint instead of the cinnamon.